They Carry a Promise

They Carry a Promise

JANUSZ SZUBER

Translated from the Polish by
EWA HRYNIEWICZ-YARBROUGH

Alfred A. Knopf · New York
2009

THIS IS A BORZOI BOOK
PUBLISHED BY ALFRED A. KNOPF

Library of Congress Cataloging-in-Publication Data
Szuber, Janusz, [date]
[Poems. English. Selections]
They carry a promise / by Janusz Szuber ; translated from the Polish by
Ewa Hryniewicz-Yarbrough.—1st ed.
p.   cm.
ISBN 978-0-307-26753-5
1. Poland—Poetry.   I. Hryniewicz-Yarbrough, Ewa.   II. Title.
PG7178.Z76A6 2009
891.8'517—dc22   2009000756

Manufactured in the United States of America
First Edition

CONTENTS

They Carry a Promise

About a Boy Stirring Jam

A wooden spoon for stirring jam,
Dripping sweet tar, while in the pan
Plum magma's bubbles blather.
For someone who can't grasp the whole
There's salvation in the remembered detail.
What, back then, did I know about *that*?
The real, hard as a diamond,
Was to happen in the indefinable
Future, and everything seemed
Only a sign of what was to come. How naïve.
Now I know inattention is an unforgivable sin
And each particle of time has an ultimate dimension.

I Began?

I began? So what that I "began."
If it's only a continuation.
Of something. Someone, someday, somewhere
Ate, breathed, fell asleep
In my name, unaware of it.
So that I would pay off his
Debts and run new ones.
In the *now* shrunken like a scrotum
After a cold bath.
Since grammar is my
Adopted country. Although
I'd prefer something less ambiguous:
The bony parachutes of leaves,
The flame of goosefoot, from a frosty page
A star bent over me.

The Clogs

The door to the entryway, hefty, with a cast-iron handle
And a barred window, ajar,
Inside dense dusk, despite the glow
On the glazed brick wall, two stone
Steps and at once the cobblestones on the street
With a fresh patch of refuse floating
In the tiny bubbles of the rainbow-hued foam.
I strain my ears and see in that dark
Oven: one, then two clogs
That stick out from under the dome of the skirts,
And with hasty steps retreat
Toward the nothingness
That lurks behind the canvas.

The Alphabet of Stones

In the middle of the ford
in Międzybrodzie
old Moshe Tieger talks
with herons and a black stork.
He flew here from a burned synagogue
on the wings of a tallith.

Why did Moshe Tieger,
blessed be his memory,
fly for over fifty years
when in a straight line
it's no more than eight kilometers
from the synagogue?

Maybe on his way in the nests
of burned towns he found
a motionless Eleatic arrow,
not a Tartar or a German one.

Strangled bundles
executed suitcases
swollen clouds—

that can't be
what Moshe Tieger looks for

in the middle of the river
lapping against the shores,
bitter with the beech
sweat of the Salt Mountains.

Letter by letter
I approach him—
my bare feet
sound the alphabet
of stones.

The Fog

The bright blue and the hard, plowed browns of
November. We passed a mound of plastic-covered silage
In the farmyard. To the south the silhouettes of the
    mountains
As if they were just forming out of dull matter,
Saturated with light at their frayed borders.
Watching out for swans wintering here,
Huge snowy peonies drifting with the current,
We drove along the river. The Orthodox church in
    Międzybrodzie
Still shone with lime whiteness
Through black rails of branches. And suddenly
The milky, thickening nothing swallowed us,
With only the pupils of the antifog lights
Above the asphalt. To tell myself to myself
As if I were those whites, browns, blues, and blacks.
Savoring the sweetness and bitterness of sounds,
Accepting pain and love and death.
To tell not myself to not myself.
Or to dream myself. To be dreamed.
Without myself in myself.

The Poor Soul

Above the lavish cascades of fabric,
Under the tree of knowledge, in the old stage sets
I danced, the poor soul, the gilded butterfly,
In the carnival mask from the *commedia dell'arte*.
What choice fruit on crystal platters!
What silverware with the monarch's intricate monogram!

The names of things and pronouns
That separate all being into I and not-I,
In what foundation were they embedded?
I approached, sniffed, fingered:
This is a table with pins and a flask of ether.
I saw myself motionless under the glass.

I was included in the collection before I was conceived,
My voracious rapture and brittle skeleton of logic,
When I squander powder in the manicured alleys
Or in the square of the ideal republic.

Everything

From high desires raptures affirmations
I built something that roughly
resembled an oil rig
reasonably solid construction
above precarious elements

and a predictable situation
a sudden gust of wind
so many degrees on the Beaufort scale
chaos terror

a broken metaphor
on a deathly pale page
tongues of flame
devouring the paper

Now I know it isn't like that
and what's worse I'm not ashamed of it
no primordial frenzy
with Shiva dancing on the cosmic ring

    between opening the window
    and making the bed
    the garish TV commercial
    and the echo of the elevator

the quiet hum of the washer
and diapers flapping on the line

you understand everything
everything

Ladybug

E.B.'s swimsuit—a red bikini
With black polka dots. For a whole decade
We said: Ladybug this, Ladybug that.
She celebrated her twenty-seventh birthday
In the oncology ward. Aware
That she had no more than one week she joked:
"Write a fable—a Ladybug and a Crab
Slept in one bed." That last
Week consisted of four and a half days.

Cocks Crowing

To Czeslaw Milosz

Cocks crowing for a change of weather:
Under the purple cloud the purple testicles of plums
With gray coating and a sticky crack—
Sweet scabs of dirty amber.

The tongue tries to smooth the coarseness of the pit
And years pass. But it still hurts the palate,
Promising that I'll touch the essence—the bottom of that day
When cocks crowed for a change of weather.

A Small Treatise on Analogy

In the car, before the synagogue in Lesko,
Waiting for Madame M.R.,
I watched a trapped bee trying
To force the slanted windshield,
Its efforts composing a simple
Parable about existence.
I picked up the notebook in which I'm
Now recording this incident, and with its help
I directed the insect toward the slightly open door,
Halfway believing that one day
Someone will treat me the same way.

Caught in the Net

For supper I ate my favorite goat cheese
Sprinkled thickly with pepper and covered with onion slices,
From a jar I forked pitted olives,
Meaty, dripping aromatic brine.

Chewing and carefully mixing all those ingredients
I felt more and more acutely my ambiguous position
Of one caught in the net, the trap, charmed by the bait,
Not even trying to possess *the ideal object.*

The Sargasso Seas

Every now and then, most often before
The weather changed, the pacing of *that something* in the
    hallway,
The distinct echo of steps, creaking boards,
The door opening on its own,
Then late in the evening the pattering in the attic
Above the ceiling, delicate, on the diagonal,
The rolling as if of balls on tin sheeting—and the feeling of
Entrapment, exhilarating, because back then
We loved to be afraid, and there was no need
To check the barometer, so the fear
Of *what was to come,* that *der Schreck*
Tasting of lemon peel grated into a sticky dough,
Before it was slid into the oven's hot abyss,
Waited for years for a complete sentence, with a predicate,
Together with the cracked glaze of the kitchen tiles,
The map for navigation exercises
Across the sargasso seas.
Yes, that was it.

Readings

When my clock neared noon
I found myself among familiar forests.
On the left the great Alighieri paced,
A tame panther bounded along his trail.
On the right a passerby from the Forest of Arden
Was choking with laughter
At the sight of foolish verses on the tree bark.

I was halfway. They were departing,
Dry twigs of berries cracked.

Maybe I am too corporeal, too grown into my body
For the promise to be fulfilled
Here where a cold cloud grows over an oak,
I thought as I walked alongside a gully
In which Heraclitus' stream murmured.

I picked up a stone. It was exactly a thing in itself.

De Se Ipso

Generous ungenerous Fate
Begrudged him talent and beauty
(While it gave in abundance
To those without merit).

He asked himself how to escape
Unscathed from the hell of physiology:
The metaphysical horror of a can
He wanted in vain to open

From inside. *All your labors*
Are like scooping water with a sieve,
An ascetic guru instructs.
Since shears will cut the thread,

The cable of the artery. Abel's breath,
A cloud of dew on the mirror,
The guardian angel your Cain will keep.
With such consolation into short eternity!

Comforted by the master's diatribe,
Through the heat proof fiber optics
Into the ear of nothingness he sent psalmodies
Like himself with no grace or harmony.

An Alley

This is like a blind alley:
When they approach armed
With brass knuckles, a wrench, or a switchblade.
Facts. The unrelenting throng of bare facts.
I, a moral fact, subject to biology.
The sky of ideas opens above me.
Here an individual pebble counts,
Each filled with itself within itself,
And I know that a plank, this one and no other,
May save me from abstraction.
Only on it grows the singular
"I am" that has been leased to me.

Klara

Testimonium ortus et baptismi:
The birth certificate of our great-great-grandmother Klara,
Maiden name Bereska, married to Hoczwa, in 1809,
Legitimately begotten, of noble birth.
Oh, those begettings on beds of rustling leaves
When wild boars forage for beechnuts
And a tin plate shines above the fog.
Here's Klara already in the clasp of birth and death—
Dressed in her body, stripped of her body,
Guarded by the motionless plaster clouds.
My heart, liver in the claws of mythology,
My large intestine, testicles *testis testimonium.*
Mine, yours, nobody's. Helpless,
Like you, Klara, more and more naked,
Dissolved in the universal, almost transparent,
I summon the possessive pronoun for help,
From the rules of grammar deriving
The necessary argument.

Councilor Rother's Trunk

A rain motif: drumming on the tin,
Gurgling in the gutters, rustling, tickling the windows
On a wooden patio where the traveling trunk
Of the late Imperial Councilor Rother rests—
A solemn sarcophagus on which, by
The glazed empty flowerpots,
Three ginger-haired cats, turquoise-eyed, sleepy and sensual,
Allowed themselves to be stroked, tolerating the tenderness
Of that someone in corduroy shorts,
Who after forty years will try
To restore a semblance of their long-past life.

The Round Eye of Weather

Shoveling coal through a window into a basement
(the frame taken off the hinges and cautiously
propped against the wall behind the gutter),
The spade scraping in the glossy pile of lumps
And lusterless dust, its polished shaft
Kneading the inside of the palm. Check the weight,
Push the right hand, heave and hurl the tumbling mass
All the way to the door down there like
A stoker in the fire room of a steamship.
Then there's Grandfather's barometer,
The round eye of weather, on the shelf in the cat's cabinet,
And an atlas with covers of frayed canvas—
In vast calcifications the wheezing lung of Africa.
Written in lowercase ports for great promises
Whispered eagerly at dawn into the ear of
A Dictaphone, when over scorched sleep,
Ulysses, tied to a mast, waits
For the sirens' salty sopranos.

Epigram

If only such a miracle would happen
For a moment or a little longer.
And I like a zaddik wrapped in the Torah,
Or maybe a pharaoh on the wall of a tomb,
When shrill constellations roar in my ears,
I'll touch *it* with my hand, lay it on my tongue,
Let it dissolve in impatient saliva.

The Lesson of Tiresias

1.

What future will oracles, talking oaks,
And divining bowls proclaim for us,
What horoscope will computers cast,
Who will be allowed to read till the end?
To what continents will dolphins
raise sunken volcanic islands?

2.

Time measured by the hourglass of a drip.
A point of light leaps on the monitor.
Who were you? A scribe, maybe a pimp.
I no longer remember. A man,
I touched snakes to become a woman.
And you, skeptics, scoffed.

3.

Give me an obol for a happy trip.
Mask my face in canvas, bandage me in psalm.
In my chart write: Recovered.
Unchain electronic dogs.
Let them track in a napalm-burned grove.
Blind, I will stare the Great Nothing in the face.

Cousin Bubi

Bubi or Caesar Roth in a Wehrmacht uniform
(the photograph the size of a postcard,
on its back a few words of dedication in gothic script),
so very boyish, the long pianist's fingers,
blond, a Nordic type, he, the son of a Polish woman from
     Drohobycz
and an Austrian Jew, a singer at the Vienna opera.
Baptized or circumcised—who cares,
let's rejoice—*mazel tov, mazel tov.* If
he were alive, how would I address him: Uncle Bubi?
The problem was solved by one of the bullets
that the Lord God, rich in mercy, carries,
fired maybe by another mutual
cousin, and Bubi was arrested in unfulfillment
at the threshold of maturity and each year
he grows younger than I.

Secondary Exhibitionism

On a folding chair, among black spruces
Where my little yellow Fiat brought me
I stared at my hand, my fingers, my nails,
Wishing to test them against the trees and clouds,
White, ragged, rushing from the south:
Here too I was separate, separate.
The pebbles from under my shoes
Flew into the ditch, the branches rustled,
I wanted to be with them, yet I couldn't
Even mock a cuckoo with my voice.
It's not true, I thought for the hundredth time, that only
Stones are sealed in their perfect skin.
And what difference does it make: in oneself or for oneself,
If separate, outside, beyond what's most important.

Geometry

Who are you? I'm one of many.
In the rigid gardens of definitions
I rake the footpaths. From unfulfillment
lame cognition came.

High and low sex? In place of gnosis
humble service to geometry. *Hosanna,*
hosanna immobile spheres sing,
alleluia the vertexes of pyramids reply.

Hłomcza 2001

For Your gifts You made us pay dearly
With pain, so beauty could grow
Like clouds, the corvettes of July clouds
Over ponds, when the southern wind
Ripples the water and the heat relents.
Then I could be in "I am,"
And what anguished me melted like
A drop of oil on asphalt, no longer mine,
No one's, returned to You
Who demands lavish payment for Your gifts.

Ashamed

He didn't even try to conceal the contradictions
within himself, and reconciled
with this state of affairs, listening for
the rumbling hoarse overture of the rutting area,
the dry clatter of the antlers, the deep
sighs and the patter of hooves, the low
gurgling of the stream, invisible from here,
looking at the withered tall white grass
and the threads of spider web, inhaling the delicate
air, here, now, at the edge of the rusty
beech forest, he, I, corporeal,
ashamed of the pain, he thought: *each pain
is mine, no theodicy will justify
its excess, this shame, only it
has remained in me unchanged for years.*
That's how in places that seemed the least
suitable he searched for the formula
of his *ergo sum.*

Mine

I was a dancer in the halls of mirrors
"I am" looked at itself in different varieties of "mine"
The possessive pronoun strengthened me in "I am"
Since "mine" without "I am" couldn't have been mine
Up above, chandeliers that someone carelessly called spiders
Lay ready to pounce
I am I but why am I this "I"
Under warm breath cool mirrors misted over

The First Verse

Long evenings when whole neighborhoods
Were blacked out to save electricity
And at home a kerosene lamp was lit:
The brass muzzle of the lamp and the smoking flame
From the turned-up wick, the lacy rim
In which the glass was mounted and me
Staring at the living, pulsating brightness,
The snorting of burning matter, the delicate
Yarn of soot, and the story of the broken lampshade,
Milky-green with a crimped ruff,
The smell of kerosene and the taste of spicy
Gingerbread, an increasingly clear
Defiance of Death with its black clock,
That breviary recited in humility and shame—
Come sentence, the first verse,
Slick or coarse, whichever, so I can
Begin now, when it's time to end.

Over a Glass of Red Wine

What was given will be taken,
What was taken is returned—
I consoled myself with that thought
Over a glass of red wine.
Dressed in jeans a girl with a spaniel
Walked up to the nearby table.
A city lived over the hedge:
Hymenoptera, membrane-winged,
A beehive swarming in the streets.

The Stormy Life of Ex-Sergeant W.

In 1847 a grievous lack of women was felt in California.
That's why Dr. Felix Wierzbicki complained
about his unmarried state and dirty linen.
With hydropathy he treated those sick of gold rush,
cut with knives and pierced with bullets.

This western has its prologue in Volhynia,
from which this underage soldier of the November Uprising
came. He was later deported by the Austrian authorities
to the United States, where he studied medicine,
allegedly in Connecticut.

Before he enlisted (arriving in California
after six months, by boat from New York), he wrote
a treatise: *The Ideal Man. Conversation between Two
Friends about Beauty, Goodness, and Truth.*

He didn't fight the Mexicans since in the meantime
the war had ended and Sergeant Wierzbicki, a private again,
left the local garrison and his superiors
with whom he couldn't come to terms.

We don't know if he searched for treasures.
He roamed on horseback and on foot,

crossed the Sierra Nevada, reached the Great Desert.
A book about the Gold Country was the outcome of that,
a best seller that went for five dollars a copy.

Maybe the defeat of the Uprising and the encyclical *Cum
    Primum*
caused his attacks on the Church and the Jesuits.
However, the doctor's true passion was metallurgy,
And until his death he worked in a San Francisco mint.

Even though he published *An Essay on the History of
    Medicine,*
he died of pneumonia at the age of forty-five,
using steam baths instead of staying in bed
and taking appropriate medications.

Mimesis

Low hills furry with forest,
Cut in the middle by a heron's even flight,
The still water in greenish ripples,
A brick house reflected flat and accurate.

Oh, I would have forgotten but I shouldn't.
A piece of foil was there, shiny, silver,
Upright among the yellowed grasses.
Moved by the wind it tried to imitate life.

Xavier

Is it possible? No, it's impossible
That out of the window of my room I now look
At the shrine to St. John Nepomucene,
Who in 1809 rescued Count Xavier
From deathly rapids and besieging Austrians,
And soaked to the bone, on a soaked horse,
He fortunately reached the castle in Lesko.

Hobbling on two crutches,
I dragged myself over to the bench, and then
One of the patients, a sincere old lady,
Read my palm: "You'll live till you're fifty."
So much longer? I was terrified.
How could I know in my twenties
That pain can also be a gift?

Is it possible that the one back then
Was me and I him? My God!
What and to whom to vow before miraculous
Arrival on that uncertain shore?

Written Late at Night

Almost all day I sat at the table
And, swapping two pens, wrote letters.
One of them, as a joke, was in gothic script.
I tried to be honest, avoid untruth
As far as the truth about myself and the events
In their general contour was accessible to me.
Then a few longer phone conversations
And a short break to read eight poems by Cavafy.
How great! Superb! Who can write like that about desire and
    love,
Admitting that when they burn out
And the bitter tasting of the body is taken away,
They guide the poet's hand. In them and only in them
All future incantations.

New Labors

I've become a pantry boy.
A job as good as any other.
I'm careful not to get my hands slapped.
I look after china sets, polish old silver
(I've never seen new silver yet).
For hours I can contemplate a ladle,
Its triumphant, inaccessible *esse,*
Which can't be possessed with words.
Different from my *I was, I am, I will,*
It arouses disinterested admiration and humility,
Respect for things existing outside me
And amazement that I've been given exactly *this*
As an advance payment for something or a promise,
Representing as it were a timid introduction
To private metaphysics.

Letter to Telemachus

I won't return into the hexameters, dear Telemachus
I won't seek revenge on the suitors and servants
I'd rather lean against the cracked wall that needs repair
than against the smoothest rail of letters

And get lost in the woods through my own error
than through the whim of the watchful snooping Gods

Now former household objects pay what they owed me
upholstered chairs a stove an indispensable table
this ballast of Phaeacian sailors that philologists have sorted
let it turn to stone fettered
by opposing currents

I'd rather die an ordinary death
than be resurrected by the will of a stranger's lips
and sway as if on a swing
at the end of someone's tobacco-smelling breath
or undigested food

So tell Mother tactfully
not to wait

Taste of Metal

Endless trouble, this wind
Here on the river, black at this time of year
When shallow ruts glazed with ice crackle.
Digging into memory as if into the crevices of a walnut
He looked for love. Love for whom or love for what.
The dog collar of the sun, a beer bottle,
And a scrap of newspaper from the past season.
By the boatman's shed locked with a hasp
A dog growled. For quite a while now under his tongue
He had felt the festive acrid taste of metal.
And his stomach kept rising in his throat
But there was no throat. Nor anything else.

The Coffin Portrait of Baron

To several generations
of bygone youngsters
he forever remained "Baron"

obese, nearsighted,
in a leather jacket

getting on his motorcycle
was an ambiguous distinction
it meant you belonged
to the Baron's stable

he loyally
paid for gas,
dents, and tickets.

> Desire like
> a barbed flame
> in the quivering
> ampulla of his body:
>
> a shard of love
> that moves the stars,

tainted by anguish
the mercy of
the earth's spirit.

Today we search for Baron
in the smoke fog ashes
lurking in the urinal
of a movie theater
or a bathhouse

the vestibule of paradise
where splendid
teenage seraphim
provocatively smiling
display their young
and supple secrets.

The Innkeeper

The innkeeper brushed the table with a napkin.
Intruders not from this epoch, though wearing its costumes,
We ordered wine and a leg of lamb,
Conscious of future events that were hidden from him,
Who lived by the measure of his calendar.

In a pewter bowl one of us laid
A bloodied wig to let the eighteenth century
Affirm itself in every detail.
We sensed at once the inappropriateness of the joke—
Accomplices, after all, in the sins of our century.

Her Fragile Profile

Like Tom Thumb or someone even smaller,
Across the cataracts of the two great wars,
Peeling old pictures from a photo album,
I wanted to sail to the beautiful epoch,

To the port where their corsets reigned,
Close to those bodies turned to ashes:
Women and girls of blood and ink.
I traveled under the sail of faded letters,

Wanting to know if she was really beautiful
In the lace of genes bestowed on me,
In dresses, combs, in the grammar of ritual,
In a plush box seat, with the thread of an aria in her ear.

Who will carve her fragile profile
In ivory and set it in ebony?
Who in truthful verse will briefly tell
of eternity, impermanent as a broken fan?

Tautologies

No revelations—only tautologies.
Even the fog from Żuków was only fog,
Lashing right up here, under the roof of the bar,
Where someone was starting stereo equipment,
And a few quiet people focused on themselves.
Before me bread, salt, bones, and a crumpled tablecloth.
In the unsaid between "already" and "still,"
They also were what they were, *idem per idem*: the rose
    of identity.

The Test of the Oak

I can't, even roughly,
tell its age: a tall, somewhat asymmetrical
oak, before Łukawica, right where the road
turns toward Monasterc and Bezmichowa.
Passing it, I always honk three times or greet it
by raising my hand. Why? I've seen some
that were more imposing, more stately.
Responsive to trees, not necessarily oaks,
I have practiced their illicit cult, putting to the test
my far from orthodox Roman Catholicism.
How to justify the choice of that and not another oak?
That and not another object of love?
The need to admire? Disinterested rapture?
The ontic imperative of choice?
Since as experience prompts,
choosing something, I choose one
possible version of myself.
I don't know. I raise my hand, I beep the horn.
The oak is losing its leaves, squandering acorns.
Bare, it greens again in late spring.

Greedy and Ecstatic

Let someone try to describe his life,
Not that he was an exception—quite the contrary:
His obsession was a relentless
Search for similarities with others.

When he sat in the parked car,
He greedily looked at them leaving
The shopping center, carting
Piles of bottles, cans, cardboard boxes,

And he imagined them in various situations,
Those hands, necks, and buttocks.
This is I, only a little differently.
And at the same time he saw their barren bones,

Tickled by the claws of sexton-beetles, and asked:
Which ones were mine?—as if in the nongrammatical,
The possessive pronoun still functioned.

It had little to do with poetry,
Yet it excited like a fortuitous sentence,
Which—maybe—would be the first verse.

To Yusef Komunyakaa

Before we meet
in mid-September
and they play blues
for us both born in 1947

I have to survive
this cruel summer
swallowing the fear and bitterness
as my sickness returns.

*

Several strained verses
this summer's only harvest
when I found *asylon*
in the old Polish town of Biecz

and conducted theological
discourses with Wacław Potocki
a seventeenth-century poet
from the Carpathians.

*

Now from your book
I'm learning you, Yusef,
an African American my age,
and repeating the incomprehensible *kadum*.

Let the devil use your head
for a drum. Since what is
to happen will happen
and no one will take it away from us.

*

Oh, how delicious, how sweet
this strawberry meringue
pie as flattened out
Katrina whirls over the Gulf.

Who'd care to look at calendars
and count the days till the end of the world?
Now there's only jazz and blues,
oh yeah, yeah, yeah, yeah.

This babe turns her eyes on you
she knows you've probed the mystery
of the smokehouse, dark places
underneath a plank, sex and death.

A plump crab runs onto the shore
dragging the seventh seal from boiling waters;
the clatter of the sunken drums
To make the most terrible gods rise out.

Birthday

He was born and then
It was too late for anything
But acting himself without himself within himself,
Since the story in which he was one of many,
By no means the most important, was to him the only
Possible form of life; thanks to it,
The *I* privileged in everyday speech
Yielded to the *he* distancing itself from him.
His fifty-seventh birthday was approaching
And at first sight there was nothing
Special about it: after fifty-six comes fifty-seven.

God Forbid

In grammar I sought *my* argument
For the sake of first and last things.
Otherwise, why write? A waste of time,
When other, more gainful occupations are at hand.
If the word can't spoon up substance
Such verse-making should go to the dogs.
A poor poem, God forbid that it ever be born.

Everything Here

The gray building of a pig farm, inside
Grunting and growling, almost black doughy mud
Through which they slogged, in squelching rubber boots,
That wet summer abounding in frogs, they worked
By accident on this farm, not quite a farm, in a poor
Region of dwarf pines and junipers,
Partly withered, at the edge of sloping
Pastures and soggy meadows, over which,
Once or twice a week, border patrols flew
In the potbellied dragonflies of helicopters, everything here,
Despite the emptiness stretching on for miles,
Barren, nobody's, was filled entirely with itself,
And when you sat over beer under the roof of that makeshift
    bar,
Without the need to prove anything,
All this had something in it that could never
Be trapped by metaphor.

Entelechy

In tennis shoes whitened with toothpaste,
Running next to a hoop steered with a stick
From the hill down the footpaths of Aptekarka park,
In the fog between familiar trees and benches,
I'd like to see myself today
Through your boy's eyes. Our shared shame
Under the duckweed of still ponds.
Above them, in that past now, the rusty sun.
Which of us more real? Who should forgive whom?
Maybe you me since I let you down.
So when you pass me busy with the hoop
I won't even try to stop you.
I'll let you keep on running.

State of Matter: Between Ice and Water

Accept it. There will never be anything else
Except this here. An April snowstorm
Sweeps away the filaments of smoke, and then
The sun appears and melting ice
Drop by drop trickles from stiff cables.
Let's avoid misunderstanding,
Stammer out this rapture together with sorrow
Between ice and water, in the hazy
Spring light when drainpipes clank.
Don't say you can't accept
This here. There will never be
Anything else in the hazy light of a snowstorm
When drainpipes clank between ice
And water. This rapture.
This rapture and this sorrow.

Farewell of Tiresias

From unexpiated guilt
Poems are born. That's why you sent
This thickening fog into my eyes.
An elevator carries me into subterranean lands—
Republics of shadow, monarchies of grayness.
The elevator attendant
Is a replica of that Theban servant-girl.
Only irritating splinters of this music of theirs
Issue from loudspeakers. Still lifes
Grow flat and cold, and I no longer
Hunger for a pear or a pomegranate.
Like a wearied gardener's dog,
I deny myself and others
the nourishment of verse.

Essay on Identity

Wild cherries, pears, and blackthorn were in bloom.
Snow still lay in mountain pastures.
Russet beech woods with a splash of purple.
The bright blue of the sky. The short wave in the lake
Lashed at the pillars of an empty jetty.
A fish and chips shop. A wooden wheel at the ceiling.
A nature preserve for young larches and birches.
After unbuckling the black safety belts,
They walked, perfectly separate, cutting transparent air.
Free, they carried previous seasons inside.
An excursion boat creaked in its fetters.
The identity of metal, varnish, concrete, and water.

To Persephone

Who will write me? Who will tell me?
Dead hedges and orchids of sperm
Arranged into bouquets by Lady Persephone?
Her kingdom, her subterranean reign,

This November and noble browns,
Low light, grays, and blackness?
Who wrote me, Persephone, who spoke me?
Who will revive a long-buried text?

The Sun in Its Milky Lampshade

The sun in its milky lampshade,
The still herons over silver-white water.
Sleepy, we walk with the antennae of the fishing poles,
Waders scraping the gravel
And prickly grass. Yesterday's
Row with the Dutchmen in the discotheque,
Agatha's tanned body asleep in a sleeping bag.
The elusive essence of the simplest
Objects and events. Another day
Of another ripe summer.
A black sinuous cat on a scratchy
Stubble field. Steaming mint,
Ravines brimful with fog.
Our steps over stones in the river.

Dybbuk

Like a dybbuk
fearing a demon,
I looked for a place to hide
and wait out bad times.

Under a thin layer
of varnish, powder, poise,
unnamed powers
tumbled and surged.

So I undid my collar
and my iron mask:
here's my soft
defenseless face.

The living to the living.
I to you. *Ich und Du.*
Your unconfessed sins
and mine.

Her body, his body,
similar, yet different,
offering a chance
at salvation.

Slight, maybe,
but still a chance.
To hide
and wait out bad times.

When I Was Fifteen

Saying goodbye, greeting.
In one incomprehensible *esse*.
Down the path along the railway embankment,
Over the water ditch thick with frog spawn.
I. For him, for her—he.

Kicking a rusty round can,
Forward, ahead of myself, to keep it
From falling into the puddle.
Or with compasses measuring the distance
Between blackened railway ties.

And so on for almost a kilometer.
All the way to a grade crossing. There a turn
Alongside the peat bog, oily, smelling of petroleum,
The road bending under the weight of my body,
Despite layers of rubble, cinders, and fascine.

Nothing special, really.
Even then obviously divided:
I, for myself also—he, walking with myself.
Separate, but at the same time in an inexplicable,
Intense union with the not-I.

A Balance Sheet

Different and yet the same
As others playing this game.
I too like others used a credit card,
a train schedule, and state insurance.
I carried urine for analysis,
and had my lungs X-rayed.

In the lottery office
I looked for my name in the list of winners.

From among medications for loneliness
the one I most often used—"Pour me
another"—turned to smoke
what was supposed to be diamond-hard.

Summoning automobile metaphors,
I could say that for years
I've driven with a broken suspension.
An ontological invalid, from the Latin
in-validus: helpless, weak, sick.

All my years empty
as tin barrels following one another,
hollow rumbling on a sloping road.

Venus above the horizon,
a pale green star with a veiled braid.
A premature widow feels the tremors
of dancing in the parquet floor
through the soles of her shoes.

Nicely said, though I know
that the unpredictable prowls incessantly
just under the surface.

Early Afternoon

We drink the cold peas of sparkling water
The bare heel bores into dust the toes raised
So many colors on them as in a peacock's tail
They stare curiously with the eyes of nails
Sparrows the gray puffs of feathers
Pluck carelessly at the jagged sidewalk
A lion stretches in a circus poster
A lady bareback rider has a pink bottom
And it smells of orange paint on the fence boards
The cold peas prick the warm palate
With silver pins and run into the throat
Like a fast train that right now
Is crouching by the platform
In the coils of gray sideburns.

Doing Inventory

Doing inventory, illuminating labyrinths with
the beam from a pocket flashlight. The one
Who speaks, within himself and to himself.
And who simultaneously hears behind the window
The shrill sound of a drill furiously boring into wood.
The one who speaks within himself and to himself,
Illuminating labyrinths with a beam of light. Drawing
Energy from a small battery in a pocket flashlight
To find, explain, and complete the inventory
Within himself. Who speaks to himself,
Not as fiercely as the shrill voice of the drill
Behind the window, beyond himself, outside.

I Had Dreams

I had beautiful dreams and was
Also happy when awake,
Always thanks to you, never
from myself in myself, so continue to be,
Now, only yourselves for me,
Like yellow flags, irises, girls by the water.

Comet

So close that it can't get closer
Since on either side lie
Virgin forests stiff from cold
Or arid fields with termitaria turrets

More fragile the boundary between me and you
A slippery comet in the slanting sky
Until so locked together that it can't get closer
We fall higher and higher greedy and defenseless

Moorlands

From there, far away an accordion rasping,
Shrill whistles of clay birds,
Sticks dancing on the plates of cymbals,
Drums tapping, trumpets squealing.

The coolness of the morning and goose bumps
On those thighs in gray shorts
Damp from low-lying, sticky fog.
Baskets of moorlands full of light.

Philology

Thickets of trochees, iambs, anapests
As if they were gooseberry, hazel, and knotgrass. Above them
Her birdlike *rrr, rrr, rrr.* We have already covered
Many divisions of Gaul, and the die has been cast.

Someone today walks streets—Chile, Bolívar—
perhaps happy, perhaps not.
*I wish I could be he.**

Our Latin teacher, Wanda K.,
An émigré from Lvov, in a summer hat
And a dress with detachable white collar,
Is just returning from the nine o'clock mass
To St. Anthony at the Franciscan church.

Blossoming mint, the smell of crab apples, they exist
As I write this, an inhabitant of the new eon,
Transforming into sentences *that something* which
Seemed unrelated to philology.

* Jorge Luis Borges, "The Exile." Translated by Alastair Reid.

Weaving into Streams

Weaving into streams
Water flows down the mountains.

I light the last of the incense sticks you made
Of willow wood dust, crushed herbs, gum,
And something else. The blue-gray smoke from a
    shaman's pipe
Soaks into the ceiling's low sky, plaster clouds.

Weaving into streams
Water flows down the mountains.

Yesterday I watched a Japanese film on TV
About Himalayan gatherers of honey from wild killer bees.
Suspended on bamboo ladders at a rocky shelf
With long poles they cut the honey-laden nests

And in tightly woven baskets lower
The priceless wax constructions.
Sticky and knotted golden strands
Trickle down smooth stones from the stubs of nests.

Weaving into streams
Water flows down the mountains.

In a letter to a friend I called myself
A Caliban in a wheelchair, who now and then squeals
In the voice of enchanted Miranda: *O, wonder! How many
goodly creatures are there here! How beauteous mankind is!*

Weaving into streams
Water flows down the mountains.

The Day Is Still Beautiful

We are on a motorcycle chugging uphill,
The three of them out of the woods, in the middle of the road,
 coming toward us:
Kaziuk, loud, with a walking stick, in a canvas field cap,
Stasia, his wife, from Vilnius—"his head hurts him"—
And Henia lugging a large basket of mushrooms.

The colors as if alive, and the three of them as if alive.
The grove in Brzozowiec hasn't thickened yet
Since that late August afternoon still continues, your
 camouflage jacket,
Your field boots, a helmet on the antlers of the handlebars.

Don't kid yourself—you know what happened next:
Senility, diabetes, and an amputated leg for her,
A stroke, paralysis, and long death for him.
And it's better not to mention the end of delicate
And refined Henia. Let her remain the way she wanted to be.

The day is still beautiful, but to your back,
Embracing you tenderly, clings Something
That used to be called fate.

Beginning of Summer

Stuffed dumplings, the best ones with
Wild cherries, small and bittersweet
In thin, almost transparent dough.
Lips smeared with cream spitting pits.
That was the beginning of summer. So what
If it was one of a kind, if it's elusive, unattainable,
No matter how often I try to renew the bond,
Establish the ritual, together with those who
Have been long in the land of Pure Essences.
I don't exist, *this is* without my *I.*
A moment, a fragment, nothing. Only
Voices, smells, clouds, wild lupine
Blooming steeply on the slopes of the Salt Mountains,
Low-flying herons above the luminous water
Of the river wound into a thick living loop.

They Carry a Promise in Coils of Smoke

You know it'll be like that to the end
Even if you no longer wonder.
Yet in spite of everything—
You could begin all over.

With a handkerchief you'll remove
A tearing spark of smoke from your eye.
The platforms through a misted window—
You could begin all over.

Yet in spite of everything,
There's so much at which to wonder
Before the last time you remove
That tearing spark of smoke from your eye.

For you and only you
The platforms through a misted window
Carry a promise in coils of smoke.
And it will be like that until the end.

Ethnographic Park

The region was wooden. A little corn,
Potatoes, oats, chickens, calves, and linen.
The girls' twin breasts smelled of russet apples.
Old women embroidering tablecloths
Didn't regret their long-dead loves.
The sun set, stars appeared.
Unconfessed sins, joyous penances.
Those tried by fate accepted its decrees.
Let the question of *unde malum* torment the insane.
The Wheel of Eternal Return creaked sleepily.
Animals ran in the streambed:
Splashy does, bushy-tailed martens.

Crossing the Threshold

A trip to the attic sprinkled with yellow
Dusty loam, a wooden tub of washed
Linen, crossing the high threshold,
Straddling the beams, enveloped in the tobacco-like
Smell, head bent, to avoid grazing
The clotheslines, water drops trickling down
Fingers when sheets and pillowcases
Were stretched, shaken lightly, and then fastened
With wooden clothespins. (Buttons
Of round tin and thread or those double ones,
Ivory colored, resembling cufflinks,
Were casually left in the dresser drawer.)
Somewhere out there was history with a capital letter,
Clouds, fathomless thunderbolts.

Ars Poetica

The poetry of the kitchen stove and its hood,
and a small leather bellows to kindle the fire,

a large brass, tarnished mortar
with a heavy, two-headed scepter of a pestle,

the ritual of the slug-heated iron
or one filled with hot coals, swinging like a censer
and tested by a finger moistened with saliva,

stoneware pots and roasting pans
mended by the widow Golda Schirtz—

all summoned to hold
close to the earth
the imagination frivolously fleeing
into regions too high.

Now

Only this grammatical usefulness
And no connection to what's beyond language.
When I utter it, I simply feel terror.
The word "now"—something that terrifies, even though
    it's tamed.

This is without question a universal feeling.
It kills itself to secure succession
Without disrupting continuity.

Futile, elusive, and we together with it,
Saying, what's more, that this is the way it should be.

I write this in case someone asks me again
About my alleged escape from the full-blooded
"Now" into the "was" posing as classicism

And this top student's complex, who follows the rules,
Minds his penmanship, never lets his notebook get
    dog-eared.

Communion of Saints

Ninety years old,
With a smoking Ducat in her cigarette holder,
My grandmother Maria
Would often stand before the portrait
Of her beautiful mother, who had died young,
Neither a woman nor a girl.
Looking at the canvas painted
In the last decade of the nineteenth century—
Its surface damaged around the amethyst brooch,
The same one that now lies in the dresser drawer—
She'd always muse: "I wonder how
We will recognize and understand each other *there*
Since judging by her looks, age, and temperament
She should be my granddaughter."

Looking at Clouds

It was hot—or blazing, as someone else might say.
Wearing maroon trunks I sat in a forest clearing
Tanning my back. Birds were making a din in the thicket,
And I couldn't peel my eyes away from the sky:
Clouds, clouds, a ballet of snowy shapes.

Time passed. Somewhere far away thunder sounded.
The peak of the mountain was across from me, and another
 more distant.
Flies were biting. The skin between my shoulder blades
 burned.
Who was I? *A consciousness residing in being?*
Myself chanced to myself, this one and not another?

A prisoner of language unable to name things
Since I instantly changed the singular into the general
And filled the outlines of things with random substance?
Then, against my will, my material "here"
Became "anywhere at all."

For the Time Being

They stand, sit, squat,
Sprinkled with confetti,
A tapestry and Marshal Piłsudski
Behind them on the wall.

In the second row, fifth from the right,
my mother Wusia Lewicka, Czesław,
Kazia, and Zdzisław, years later a prelate,
Here in a high school uniform.

And the whole family of Judge Fried,
In curls or wearing ties, as if
The hurriedly dug hole in the Jewish cemetery
No longer waited for them.

For the time being they are
Between one dance and another,
Without barbed wire,
A bullet in the back of the head,
Births in cellars,
And the word "exile."

And if there's a number,
It's a short one on a school badge.

In a few days from Stachocki's
Photography studio they'll pick up
This photo with the serrated edge.

Nihil Esse. After Zeno of Elea.

Why scaredy-cat?
I wasn't afraid of the dark room,
And subjected to the test of a rusty nail,
With a bleeding thigh, I looked into her eyes
As if nothing had happened,

While the itching trickle flowed
Straight into my sneaker (who'd
Wear socks in such heat?)

And when at last I had too much,
I ran upstairs, staining the wooden steps,
A student of second grade, section A, never in B,
All through school until graduation.

Almost half an age after that
I attempt a transfusion of that blood
Into those familiar words. And what?
A white page, black ink. Nothing.

Andy Warhol

Less than an hour's drive from me to you, Andy.
On the way a few mountains we share as neighbors.
Above them clouds, let's say the July clouds,
Flocks of feathery peonies summoned here
From the wise Book of Zen.

I'm eating a banana that I picked off your head,
And its taste will do for the discourse
On the art of the past century.
If someone says I copped out writing the above,
He will most likely be right.

Skinny, under an umbrella with only
Wires remaining, you stand stiffly opposite
The frothy Orthodox church
Fit for Disneyland.

In your honor, Andy, I shuffle postcards
I bought for my friends in your museum,
Proof of how easy it is for us now
To cross borders.

Coming to the Shore

Coming to the shore, undoing
The shoelaces on the last rocks,
Pulling off the socks, the bare feet,
The first, the second, the fourth, they walk
On concrete slabs washed by the river,
Into unceasing rumble, throaty sounds,
To the other side, with clumps of alders,
Gray willow, and steaming hay.
My knowledge—my ignorance. And how
Should I have known? The others somehow knew,
Equipped maybe with an additional sense,
And sure of themselves out in the open, they accepted
    the touch
Of water as something ordinary and were given
Grace that I was denied.

Childhood Refrains

My mother's great love was
the cinema. So instead of fairy tales
she told me movies from the thirties.
I remember her still maiden drawer
full of photos and so-called circulars

And that in our county seat
Second Lieutenant Karwasiński
from the Second Regiment of Mountain Riflemen
was a serious competitor
for passionate screen lovers.

My mother and her sister Krystyna
took English lessons under the Nazi occupation
from Dr. Jan Świerzowicz.
Mother, it seems, so that after the war
she could pronounce correctly
the first and last names
of Hollywood movie stars.

It makes sense to summon
here in the fourth stanza
another refrain of my childhood,
namely: what would have happened
if not for nineteen thirty-nine.

Surely it would have been "better" than "worse"
since "the worse" already exists,
and continues slipshod and grayish,
with a Tartar's pockmarked
and moronic face.

These two things together made me
often lose sense of what
belonged to fiction
and what to reality.

Only thanks to writing poems
I felt solid ground under
my feet at last.

In the Third Person Singular

It's still dark, so he lights the lamp.
He looks first at what he's looked at
many times, the same pants, T-shirt, briefs,
the way he left them on the chair.
He reaches for a writing pad
and a pen so that what recurs
and seems necessary will find
confirmation in the declarative mood.
What if, for instance now, close by,
facing the wall, he or she,
her clothes or his got mixed with those
here on the chair? Then what?

Tire and Gravel

On the highway through the woods to the mountain pass.
Along the road's shoulder logs from beech trees cut last
    winter.
On the other side of the pass a valley
With the froth of blossoming apple trees.

The asphalt ends. Farther down a stony road
all the way to the river. Close to the shore a canoe
for crossing to the other not so distant shore.

To be myself. Here and now.
With nothing inessential.
Telling the tire on the gravel
and the gravel. Above vaulted cellars,

in which at the bandmaster's order
deaf instruments have been laid.

Pronouns

For him and for those like him
Here in this forever and ever,
The fiery cigars of the harbingers of the Apocalypse
And multistoried tsunamis rolling
Toward the beaches of paradise islands.
Black boxes stubbornly silent,
Black holes and these their pronouns
Useless there, in the nongrammatical.

Everyman

Someone spoke in his place about him: he, his, him,
When he was rinsing soap off his own familiar body,
After watching the TV news
Pierced by the resounding lament
Of some strange women and ambulance sirens.
He wrote poems and a few read them,
But that's no reason to be full of hot air.
On the contrary, Empress Statistics
Also reigned here with the help of numbers.
Till the crack of dawn in the square outside his window
Someone else beat the drum and the throaty laughter
Could have been his.

ACKNOWLEDGMENTS

The following poems have been previously published, sometimes in slightly different form:

"Geometry," "Everything," "The First Verse," "Over a Glass of Red Wine," and "Greedy and Ecstatic" in *Absinthe*

"About a Boy Stirring Jam" in *Boulevard*

"Hłomcza 2001" and "I Began?" in *Image*

"The Fog" in *The New Yorker*

"Taste of Metal" in *The Literary Review*

"Cocks Crowing," "The Clogs," "The Round Eye of Weather," "The Poor Soul," "Cousin Bubi," "The Innkeeper," "Councilor Rother's Trunk," "The Sargasso Seas," "Secondary Exhibitionism," and "A Small Treatise on Analogy" in *New Orleans Review*

"Klara" in *Poetry*

"Entelechy," "Everything Here," and "State of Matter: Between Ice and Water" in *Ploughshares*

"De Se Ipso" and "New Labors" in *Post Road*

"An Alley," "Xavier," and "Readings" in *Seneca Review*

"Crossing the Threshold" in *Threepenny Review*

A NOTE ON THE TYPE

The text of this book was set in Century Schoolbook, one of several variations of Century Roman to appear within a decade of its creation. The original Century Roman face was cut by Linn Boyd Benton (1844–1932) in 1895, in response to a request by Theodore Low De Vinne for an attractive, easy-to-read typeface to fit the narrow columns of his *Century Magazine*.

Composed by North Market Street Graphics, Lancaster, Pennsylvania

Printed and bound by Thomson-Shore, Dexter, Michigan

Book design by Robert C. Olsson